Please Don't Beg

How To Get Book Reviews And Keep Your Friends

By Keith Wheeler

©2018

Don't just stop with reviews.

Get your FREE copy of

13 Ways to Promote Your Book!

http://www.kwheelerbooks.com/p/13ways.html

Intro

In general, I despise intros to books. To be honest, most of the time I completely skip over them. Why? Because when I spend my hard earned money on a book or ebook, I don't want to waste 30-40 pages hearing about why the author wrote the book, all of their credentials and why I should listen to them. Just get me into the "meat and potatoes" of the subject! What do I need to learn?

So, here is my promise to you:

1.) I will show you practical ways to get book reviews without begging!

2.) I will tell you what to do(or not do) to get those reviews to work for you and why.

Now, enough of the intro crap, let's get started!

Why Are Reviews Important

This is such an important question and most authors have very strong feelings one way or another about this.

At its core, book reviews are, simply put, the opinions of individual readers about a specific book. Just like you may ask friends, family and acquaintances their opinions when you're considering buying a new car or moving to a new neighborhood, book reviews allow potential readers to get customers insights into a book, prior to making a purchase.

As for the level of importance of book reviews to the overall success of a book, there are several different "camps" authors belong to.

Some believe that the most important driving force to the success of your book is the number of reviews. The more reviews you have, the "better" your book will sell. This mentality is backed up by the fact that Amazon and other sales sites, use customer reviews in their algorithm that controls where on the search page your book is displayed when a potential customer does a search. The more reviews, the higher on the page your book will be displayed. However, based on detailed research that I've done, it appears that the actual **relevancy** of your book to that particular keyword holds a much higher importance in the sites algorithm than the number of customer reviews you have. Although, they do appear to factor in.

At the other end of the spectrum are the authors that feel that reviews do absolutely nothing for the sales of your book and if you simply "write a good book", the book will "sell itself". I too can understand this mentality, as it is true that most of your time should be spent in writing your book. Spending your time writing and editing your book, as well as bringing in some beta readers, helps to increase the quality of your manuscript. As logic dictates, the better the book, the better your chances of getting honest, organic reviews.

And you guessed it, as with anytime you have two polar opposite opinions on a topic, there is a third view which is a combination of the two. This group believes that, while reviews are important to get the customer insight into your book, you should not spend all of your energy focused on getting every possible review you can. Your time is better spent "writing your next book."

SO WHICH VIEW IS CORRECT?

All of them! Just as there are multiple authors views on book reviews, customers views differ, as well. There are customers that ONLY buy books that contain lots of reviews. They feel that if a book doesn't have reviews or doesn't have "enough reviews", then it must not be a good book. On the other hand, there are also customers that completely ignore customer reviews on books. They take a look at the cover, description, price and, if it's there they may check out the look inside feature, and use all of that info to decide whether or not to purchase the book. Then of course, you guessed it, there are customers who do a little of both. These individuals read reviews, however, do not rely solely on reviews to make their purchasing decisions. It is just one tool that they use in their arsenal to make an educated decision on whether or not to purchase a book.

So how you want to view and handle reviews for your book depends a great deal on your book, your author platform and your long term ambition as an author.

If you are a well-known author with a large platform, you most likely do not need to worry about getting reviews, because your name and reputation are enough of a driving force to get your books sold, most likely in mass quantities. Your organic reviews will come in on their own and there's very little need to spend a lot of time focusing on how to squeeze out every single review you can find. That said, if you're truly that well known, you're probably not "wasting your precious time" reading this book.

Now, if you wrote a crappy book and you're just hoping to "milk the system" to get some sales, then, yeah you're probably going to need all of the 5 star reviews your mom and friends can give you. Although warning, polishing a turd is still a turd! Although you may trick people into buying your book, they will most likely retaliate with HONEST reviews, which will not only quickly place your book back to the gutter where crappy books belong, but could also feel the wrath of Amazon, who care deeply about their customers and the quality of the products they receive.

So your best bet is to write a good book AND try to get some reviews. Not paid reviews, but honest customer reviews. Now I know that seems easier said than done, but I will do my best to help navigate you through the review search journey while keeping your sanity intact.(or at least the sanity you started with!)

Knowing that and, more importantly, accepting that, is key to the success of your book and your longevity as an author.

Where To Get Reviews

When most authors think of getting book reviews, they almost always, instinctively think of Amazon. That makes perfect sense, because they are such a huge force in the online sales world. While I agree that Amazon IS a place you want to ask for book reviews, you definitely don't want to limit yourself to just one platform for getting reviews. There are many more places to consider getting book reviews and I suggest try to at least a few reviews on as many of them as possible. Your potential readers are all over the world and all over the internet, so you want you and your books to be just as widespread.

For starters, even within Amazon, many of the countries that your book is available in(even if it's not translated), has its own separate Amazon site or at least a site for that area. Italy, Spain, Canada, Australia and the UK are just a few of the alternate Amazon sites that are available. Each of these sites can host reviews from customers who bought your book from that countries site.

In addition to other countries, every format and platform that you have your book available on will most likely have their own product review system. This includes Kobo, iBook, Nook, Scribe, etc. Be sure to reach out to these customers and request them to post their honest reviews. You want all of your readers to know that their opinion and experiences with your book are important to you.

Don't forget about audio. If your book is available through Audible or other audio sites, they too will most likely have their own review system in place. Audiobooks are a rapidly growing area for book sales due to consumers busier schedules and longer work commutes. These individuals are extremely passionate about their books, so be sure to capture that passion, in the form of book reviews. In addition, some other possible places for reviews are sites like Goodreads, blogpost reviews, local newspapers, magazines, community forums and groups, work or church newsletters, etc.

Also, it is easy to forget about the one place that most people spend at least a few hours a day, and that is social media. If you have a Facebook page for you or your book, there is usually a place where people can post reviews. The possibilities are endless. Anywhere your readers may be, that's where you want your book reviews to be found, as well. I'm sure if you just go about your normal week, you could jot down a few more places that you visit, either on or off-line, that I didn't even mention.

What To Do With The Reviews

The next question an author may ask is 'what do I do with the reviews once I have them?' This is an excellent question. Getting reviews is great, but what you do with them once you have them is what makes an author really stand out.

The average author will just let the reviews come in and leave them on the platform and do nothing else with them. While the reviews on the platform may help in drawing attention to you and your book, this is a huge missed opportunity. Especially when you receive 4 and 5 star reviews, you want to share this info in as many places as possible. What's the sense in having a nice, shiny car if you don't show it off, right?

Remember, from the previous chapter, where ever your potential readers are, that's where you want your reviews to be. So, if they don't or can't leave reviews on your social media page or website, take the reviews they left somewhere else and share them there. Share them wherever you can.

For example, if you have a 4 or 5 star review on Amazon or another platform's site, take that review, either via direct quote or screen shot, and post it on your website. I actually suggest that you create a 'Reviews' page on your website where you repost reviews from all over. If you get interviewed or reviewed in a magazine or local newspaper, take a picture of it and post it on your website. Also don't forget the international sites. Nothing gives you better momentum than showing that people from all around the world love your book.

You can also take those same 4 and 5 star reviews and post them on all of your different social media. Now, when you have multiple reviews that you want to post or repost, instead of posting them all at once, spread it out over a few days, weeks or even better, months. Showing a consistent amount of positive reviews, over a long period of time, brings in way more traffic than blasting it all over social media over a matter of hours.

Another great place to reuse your positive reviews is on your Goodreads and Amazon books pages. You can take the reviews from normal customers and add them into your description for that particular book. If your book was reviewed in a newspaper, magazine or even on someone else's blog page, you can add those in as "editorial reviews". Just be sure to state where the review came from and credit the reviewer.

If you have an especially positive review or from a very reliable or popular source, create media that takes advantage of this. For example, if your book was reviewed by USA Today or a blogger says that your book is the best book they've read in that genre in years, perhaps create book marks for your book and include this quote on them. This will add some authenticity and originality to your book. Then, once you've created these, give those bookmarks out at book signings or use as additional prizes in your next giveaway. I'm sure, if you put your creative thinking cap on, you can come up with some really original ways to use these bookmarks.

You can take this same mentality when it comes to other media. Using free or inexpensive software, you can create one page flyers that include the image of your front cover, a few examples of your best reviews and a link and/or QR code to your books sales page. Don't forget to include the author headshot from your media kit and you now have a flyer that you can print out and provide to any bookstores or shops that have agreed to carry your book. With a little chat from the store manager you can probably arrange to create a unique flyer tailored to that specific store and their clientele. Don't be afraid to ask, because remember, the more of your books they sell, the more money they make.

While you're at it, reach out to the store manager and see if they're ok with you creating a unique book trailer that advertises your book being sold at their store. Throwing out words like "advertises" or "features" are trigger words that will usually catch their attention and typically will lead to a very excited yes. The bottom line is you're creating a commercial, of sorts, for their store, that they don't have to pay for. The worst they can say is no, so give it a shot.

You can also take reviews that specifically compliment your writing abilities and post those on your authors pages. These targeted reviews help add validity to you as an author as a whole. They help you to stand out from the crowd and, since it's about YOU and not the specific book itself, you can use these reviews on ALL of your media, regardless of the book you're promoting. While readers may love a specific book, it's when they reference your ability as a writer, that will really make you shine. Again, also remember to share this positive information on the main page of your website as well as on your social media author page.

Eventhough your book is completed and already live on the internet and possibly even in brick and mortar outlets, once you've acquired a decent number of exemplary reviews, you might consider updating the cover of your book to include those extremely positive comments. Now, if you're going to take the time to update your cover, make sure that the reviews you include really stand out, not just a nice 'I really liked this book' review. Any reviews that are in depth, detailed or draw from emotions should be considered when deciding which ones to put on the new cover. If the review is from a very reliable, well-known source, be sure to include that review on the front cover of the book. This will catch the potential readers attention right from their first glance.

Who To Ask

Let me start off by telling you who NOT to ask. The days of asking your parents, grandparents, aunts, uncles and second cousins, twice removed, is long gone. That tactic may have worked a few years ago, but outlets like Amazon have caught on to that and to be honest, so have readers. When you read a review you can tell if it's from a friend or family member or some other person with some vested interest as oppose to an authentic reader.

Now, I know there are tons of authors that have done this tactic and have gotten away with it. Or should I say, have gotten away with it…so far! Just because they haven't gotten caught yet, does not mean that they're in the clear. Amazon and sites like them run constant checks on reviews and accounts. It's just a matter of time before their luck runs out. I've seen many amazing authors lose all of their reviews just because of one or two questionable ones. And once an author is 'caught', I've seen them lose their abilities to post reviews on products themselves as well as even losing the ability to comment on reviews to their own books. It's simply not worth it.

In addition, asking friends and family to buy and review your book can actually have a negative effect on your long term book sales. When sites like Amazon use their algorithms to determine which customers to advertise your book to in their "recommendations" listings, etc. they use data science to determine who your "target audience" is. Meaning, they look at who's bought your books and what they all have in common. So, if you have friends and family buy and review your book, since they're not really your target audience, they're throwing off the algorithm. The end result is, if the system can't find a similarity between your customers, they don't know what "type" of person to advertise it to. Therefore, the system simply doesn't advertise it. So, what you thought was helping you, could actually hurt you in the long run.

Similarly, I suggest staying clear of the "paying for reviews" and "review swapping" type of behavior that so many "experts" seem to be spouting out as being ok. The bottom line is it's cheating the system, and while you're more than welcome to take any practices you'd like, I strongly advise against this. And just to be clear, hiring a virtual assistant or VA to do this for you is not saving you or shielding you from the responsibility. In the end, it's your book, your reputation and, in some cases, your livelihood on the line. In my opinion, it's just not worth the risk, especially when there are so many other, honest ways to get reviews.

Now that that's out of the way, it's time to get to the question at hand, 'Who do I ask for reviews?' The answer is simple, you know the few people I listed about who not to ask…ask everyone else. Obviously, if you have a newsletter or other author platform, you want to reach out to them. Let them know that you have a new book and that you'd love HONEST reviews.

The first place I always reach out to when it comes to reviews is to the biggest reader in my neighborhood, the librarian at the local library. If your book is a children's book, reach out to the librarian's at all of the schools in your area that cater to the age group your book is written for. My next stop would be my local bookstores. Not only will I reach out to them to possibly sell my books, but chances are at least one employee there is an avid reader and looking for their next book to read. Bookstores and librarians are also usually a great source of information. They typically will know of any reading groups that gather in your area. The members of these groups are another great source of potential readers and reviewers. Teachers, especially English teachers, are also a great source of reviews and/or insight as to local groups. You can even offer to hold a contest for their students and perhaps be willing to guest speak on the 'life of an author'.

The key is to know your target audience, where and how they consumer their reading material and then reach out to them in that same manner. If your book is historical in nature, you'd want to reach out to history teachers, any historical society in your area, as well as historical groups online, including social media. Nowadays, there are numerous groups for any possible topic you can think of on each social media platform. Find out where your readers are and seek them out.

Speaking of social media, there are also groups on most social media platforms that are just looking for books to read, regardless of the subject matter. Be sure to reach out to these groups, introduce yourself and your book and gauge the interest in your book. If they're not interested, move on to the next group. Make sure that you're not just popping in, asking for reviews and then leaving. You should try to plan ahead and become a somewhat active member in the group. If people in that group are familiar with your name and the input you've shared with the group, they are way more apt to read and review your book.

Another group of people who love to read and also understand the importance of reviews, are other authors. Now I know I just got through saying NOT to review swap, and I meant it. But asking an author to read and review your book, with HONEST reviews, is not review swapping. At that point, the author is just another customer. It only becomes questionable when you review their book in exchange. I will give you some suggestions, later in the book, on ways to legitimately navigate these treacherous waters, but for now, know that having another author read and review your book is ok.

While I do suggest against having friends and family review your books, that does not mean that they cannot talk to their friends and colleagues (people that would honestly be interested in the book and genre) and ask them to read and review your book. Chances are, if you wrote a romance novel and you "know" Aunt Sara loves romance novels, she probably knows other people who read that same genre of books as well. A referral from her might be all you need to get another person to check out your book.

How To Ask For Reviews

So, we've covered who to ask, where to ask and even what to do with the reviews once you've got them, but one of the hardest aspects of getting reviews that authors run into is, HOW to actually ask for the review. You don't want to come off needy or pushy or flat out desperate. So, how do you ask a stranger to write a review for a book that you've poured your heart and soul into? The truth is, it's actually pretty easy. Now, I didn't say it will come natural or that it will not be uncomfortable at times, but my goal is to try and ease your reluctance and give you a strong, working foundation for getting the ball rolling.

First, you want to be honest and authentic. People are inundated on a daily basis by other people who want them to buy things or do things for them. Whether it's a telemarketer, a charitable foundation or the kids asking what's for dinner, people are prone to be on the defensive, right off the bat. So, the most important thing you can do is just be honest. You can do this simply by explaining the importance of reviews not only for the author, to help them and their book get noticed, but also explain how honest reviews provide valuable information to potential purchasers and can greatly help them in the decision whether or not to purchase a particular book.

Now, I know that the thought of explaining this to someone, especially someone you don't know, sounds like the exact opposite of natural and, if you were thinking that too, you'd be correct! I'm not talking about explaining, verbally, to someone the importance of reviews, although you can do that if you'd like. I'm actually talking more about what your "message" is going to be and then putting that message on all of you marketing material.

Just to be clear, I'm not saying that you need to have some lengthy explanation as to what a review consists of and list endless examples of how it aids in the discoverability of a book and the author on countless platforms, blah, blah, blah. No way! If you wrote that, you'd have lost me after the first sentence. I write mostly children's books for a reason. That's where my maturity level and attention span peaked. If you don't believe me, ask my wife. Think about the most memorable slogans and catchphrases you've run into over the years. The one thing you'll find they all have in common is that they are short, sweet and to the point. Your "message" should follow this same methodology. If a 10 year old can remember it, than so can your customers.

Your message should be something like, "Help an author, leave a review!" or "Read, review, repeat!" Something that will catch their attention, make them think, make them laugh, but most of all, make them REACT! A really great message would be if you could integrate the name of your book into your message. For example, one of my children's picture book series is called the "My Buddy Knows" series and it teaches letters, numbers, colors and shapes for preschool aged children. With this in mind, a great "message" for me would be "My Buddy Knows that Happiness Starts with Reviews!" or "My Buddy Knows that Reviews Start with 5 Stars!" If you have written a novel that draws the reader in, writing a little blurb as if it's coming from one of the main characters asking for a review, can really impact your reader. "Want to go on more adventures with me? Leave a review and let me know!"

Now that you have your message, you want to include this "message" inside your book. I mean, let's be honest, if they're already in your book, where better to ask for a review. Most authors that include this in their book, do so at the very end of the book. They take the last page and put a review request blurb/message. While I do think this is a good idea, an even better idea is to ALSO put this message or a similar one at the beginning of the book. This will get the readers already in the mindset to leave a review and then the reminder at the back of the book will help drive the message home. Also, many people, especially those reading ebooks, don't actually finish the book, therefore, those people would never have gotten to your end of the book "message". But if you also included it at the beginning, the seed has been planted to review the book, even if they haven't finished it.

Like I said previously, you also want to include this "message" in all of your marketing material. On the back of your business cards you can include a shortened version of your review importance "message". In addition, you can include the link to the Amazon or other sales page. If you want to take it a bit further, you can create a QR Code that brings them to your book's sales page. QR Code readers are free to download on smartphones and are much easier than typing out an entire url. Also, many people today are reluctant to use 'shortened' url links, so a QR code could be a very affective substitute. Remember, you want to make the book review process as easy on your readers as humanly possible.

Another great way to ask for reviews is, when you're on social media and you're making a post that shares one of your great reviews, add a comment that says something along the lines of "Be the next review of the week", and then remember to post the link to the book. You want to make leaving a review sound interesting and desirable. The more people think they'll get out of it, the more likely they are to do it. The temptation of their review being posted on social media, may be enough to spark some interest.

Do you have an author's website? If you don't, I strongly suggest you get one. On the front page of the site include an image of all of your books along with links on where your visitors can buy them. In addition, I suggest that you create a "Review" page on your website. On the review page you'll include most, if not all, of your best reviews. Then, at the bottom of the page you'll include links for all of your books, so the visitors can go back and review them. You can also add a tag that says something along the lines of "Leave a review and YOURS could be the NEXT FEATURED REVIEW!" Again, make it sound like a reward. Human beings in our society have a 'What's in it for me?' mentality, so use that to your advantage. Tell them right off the bat what's in it for them, and you could be happily rewarded.

How To Utilize Social Media

Social media is everywhere around us these days. We use social media to keep in touch with friends and relatives and even that really annoying kid from 10th grade. You know the one with the funny haircut. So with all of the time we spend on social media, why not tap into those outlets to try and get some more book reviews?

Now, I've already mentioned how you can take some of your best 5 star and even some of your 4 star reviews and share them on your different platforms, but that's just the tip of the iceberg. Different strategies can be used depending on what social media platform you're using. Platforms like Goodreads have forums created for the sole purpose of reaching out to authors and allowing them to post links to their books that they would like HONEST reviews for. While, it's true that most of these forums are designed for authors to provide a FREE copy of their book to be read and reviewed, I look at that as a good thing. You can't be accused of 'buying reviews' if you gave the book for free, right? Just be sure to reiterate that you're looking for honest, voluntary reviews. Also, understand when I say 'give away a free copy' it typically means you're giving away a digital copy, so there's really no money lost on your part. While you can't really force the reader to review the book after they get it, you're basically playing the numbers. The more people who have access to your book, the greater your chances of getting a book review.

Other platforms, like Facebook have different groups that you can join. There are groups for every possible book genre, sub-genre and niche. There are even groups set aside based on the format of the book. So you can search for 'children's picture ebook' and you will find groups and posts related to that specific topic. Once you find a group that you feel might be interested in your book, reach out to them and offer a free digital copy. Don't even ask for a review. If you followed the other suggestions I've provided, you already have a reference to giving reviews inside your book.

Another great place to ask for reviews on social media is by taking advantage of the yard sale/marketplace type groups and forums and post an ad there. Again, you're offering it for free, so most sites will not mind you posting a link there. If you feel the need to ask for a review with the link, keep it simple and non-pushy. Something like, "Honest reviews welcomed." Again, you're playing the numbers, the more groups, forums and platforms you post your requests in, the greater your chances of reviews.

If your book is a non-fiction book, then an often overlooked platform would be LinkedIn. If you're not familiar with it, LinkedIn is a professional/business oriented social media platform. Just like the other platforms I've mentioned, LinkedIn has groups and forums with a wide variety of topics. So, if your book is about accounting, for example, you would definitely want to reach out to those groups on the platform.

With most social media, images are extremely helpful, so when you post a link to your book, if cover image isn't automatically displayed, be sure to include one, on your post. You can also, periodically, share other images or excerpts from your book on your social media sites. You want to use images or excerpts that will entice them to click the link and check out and possibly review your book.

Now I know you might be saying, 'Wait the title of the book says 'Please DON'T Beg' and now you're telling me to go all over social media and beg and plead for reviews. Let me be clear, there is a huge difference between begging and requesting. Begging is when you approach someone who has absolutely no interest in you, your book or even the topic of your book, and you ask them to read and review your book. Because these people honestly have no vested interest, this also usually leads to the need to ask or remind these people over and over again until they either give in or change their number. The worst part about begging is not only is it humiliating, but most of the time the end result is either a generic 'I like the book' review or no review at all.

Requesting, however, is completely different. What we're talking about in this book is reaching out to specific groups of people with specific interests that will benefit from your book, even if they don't know it yet. Because these people are interested in this topic and/or genre, they will be more naturally apt to actually read the book and, perhaps, leave a review. What does this mean? It means much less work on your part with a much higher chance of return.

How often you post, requesting reviews, is also a very touchy subject. While there is no set formula, I would say the less frequently you do it, the better your chances of responses. So when you do it, make sure you do it right. Instead of just posting on Facebook asking for book reviews, make it an interactive event. Make the members in the group or forum or on your page feel invested. For example, instead of saying "Here is a link to my book, reviews welcomed", you could post something more interactive like, "I've recently received my 24th book review for [book name]. Help me find review number 25!" See how this latter request is a lot more enticing? Interest leads to action!

One more thing you want to take into consideration with regards to review requests on social media, is the speed at which posts are being made. This will help you gauge how often to repeat a request in the same day. Obviously, on a site like Facebook, you can post a message or a "book review count" post once, maybe twice in the same day. On the other hand, a more fast paced site like Twitter will need to be reposted numerous times throughout the day to ensure it is seen by all of your followers.

Also, don't forget to use hashtags. Studies show that posts with hashtags are seen, interacted with and shared more frequently than posts that do not include hashtags. That said, most experts will agree that more than 5 hashtags begins to deter people. So pick a few, relevant hashtags and include them on all of your posts.

Why Use ARC Readers

ARC readers are another great way to get book reviews. Let me start off by explain what an ARC reader is. ARC is short for Advanced Readers Copy. These readers are people that get copies of your book before it's published. Typically, these readers act as an author's last form of proofreading, prior to deploying the book to the general public.

Before you decide to completely skip this section because you don't write novels, understand that ARC readers are not just for lengthy manuscripts. I, personally, use ARC readers for my children's picture books. Children's books are especially difficult, as you have a lot fewer words to project your story. Therefore, you need to make sure that you use clear and precise verbiage to get the most possible impact from your story. For this exact reason, ARC readers can make or break the success of your book. While I'm not saying you have to have ARC readers, I AM saying that getting someone interested and familiar with the genre and their tropes, and having them review your book can help dramatically. Remember, just like with an editor, you don't have to make every single change they suggest, but they may bring up items that you wouldn't have otherwise thought of or noticed.

When deciding on an ARC reader you don't just want fans, you want super fans. People that are willing to take the time to read your book and help you to make it better. If presented right, you should have people jumping at the opportunity to read your book before everyone else gets ahold of it. Many times you can even get away with sending them only a digital copy of the book, which means it costs you virtually nothing, while gaining not only a free proofreader, but also some early reviews.

Before selecting someone as an ARC reader you should make sure that your book is in a genre and a topic that they'd be interested in reading. You also want to make sure that they have the time in their schedule to devote to thoroughly reading your manuscript. One thing that I do when selecting readers, especially for a series, is that I require that they have read, and liked, the other books in the series. This ensures that they're familiar with your storyline, tempo and mood of your story as well as just your overall writing voice. The reason why I make sure they liked the other books in the series is that, if they didn't like the others, there's a greater chance they won't like this one and let's be honest, one of the main purposes for getting an ARC reader, is to get positive reviews.

On that note, you should also make sure that they understand that part of their job as an ARC reader is to, when the book goes live, post an honest book review on whichever platform you dictate. One thing to keep in mind is that you should not require that they post reviews on more than 2 sites, although you can ask for more. In addition, depending on the number of ARC readers you use, you should space out the posting of the reviews over multiple days. Also, to ensure you don't get flagged by book sales pages, make sure you tell the ARC readers, to state in their review that they received an advanced copy of the book in exchange for an HONEST review.

Now, full disclosure, some of your ARC readers may not actually leave reviews as requested. I know it's hard to believe but there are some people out there that are just interested in getting free things and then moving on. In fact, they may not have even read your book. Unfortunately, there's really nothing you can do about that, except make sure that they are on your DO NOT USE list for future ARC readers lists. The good news is that you only sent them digital copies of your book so you're not really out any money. Just focus on those readers that lived up to their end of the agreement and read and reviewed your book.

Instead of focusing on the negative, I prefer to reward the positive. For all of my ARC readers that followed through on their part, I reward them by sending them a signed copy of the book with a personal message thanking them for their efforts. Your ARC reader list should be one of your most prized possessions. It doesn't matter if you only have 1 ARC reader, cherish them. The more your platform grows, so will your pool for choosing ARC readers.

As you look to add more ARC readers, use your gut, previous reviews, as well as social media, to find your candidates. That fan that comments on almost every post you make on social media, the person who leaves messages on your website asking questions about your books and readers who have left positive reviews on your previous books, are all great places to find your next ARC reader.

If all else fails and you can't find any viable options in the places above, simply put a post on your website or social media asking for ARC readers. Also, be sure to mention that there are only a few spots available. By adding this "sense of scarcity" you increase not only your chances of getting inquiries, but you also speed up the rate in which the requests come in. People love to get free things, as well as love to feel like their opinion is important and being listened to.

Once you have your potential candidates, then create a brief questionnaire(1-4 questions), just to make sure you pick readers that will be a good fit for you and that specific book. You may find someone that is a great fit for you but maybe not a great fit for that specific book that needs to be reviewed. That's why the questionnaire is so important. You don't want to waste a great reader on a book that just won't interest them. Just ask them if you can add them to your list of ARC readers for a future book that may suit them better.

Unless you have a huge following, I would suggest limiting your ARC reader list to 1 to 10 readers. Start off small with just 1-3 and then as you continue to produce books you can add to and remove from the list, based on whether or not they followed through on their part. Also, if you write in more than one genre or more than one type of book in that genre, you'll want a separate list for each type of book. While you may have some readers make it onto multiple lists, it is imperative that you keep your lists separate. You can quickly turn off a great ARC reader by giving them a book that they're not interested in or at least get a not-so-great review from them.

Also, understand that you're asking these people for HONEST reviews, which means that just because they give you a questionable review does not mean you should remove them from your list for future books. Decisions like this should be made based on the content of the review. If they say something like "this book wasn't for me..." then you should reach out to them and make sure that they're really interested in your genre and sub-genre. Also, if you send your ARC files out early enough, these readers can help you fill any holes, fix typos, etc. before the book goes public. If you listen to their feedback and make these adjustments or at least consider them and respond back and let them know why you didn't make the adjustment, you should get a larger number of positive reviews.

Reaching out to them in regards to their feedback is an extremely important aspect that should not be overlooked. These people are offering up their time to help you make your book better, both in content as well as in early reviews. So, be sure to let them know their input is important to you. Even if you don't implement the suggestions that they made, letting them know that you understand what they're asking for and explaining why you chose not to make the change will go a long way to building a symbiotic relationship. Add to that, the appreciation you show when they follow through with their reviews by sending them a thank you card or signed book and you'll have an dedicated ARC reader.

Think of ARC readers as virtual employees. Happy, dedicated ARC readers are your ideal end game. For starters, the more dedicated ARC readers you have, the less time you have to spend finding replacements. These readers are basically free proofreaders, but with a twist. While normal proofreaders just look at the text, these readers are familiar with your genre so they may catch issues that are not wrong textually, but wrong in relation to how they compare with other books in that genre or sub-genre. Also, a dedicated ARC reader will typically leave you a better review and will leave it in a timely manner after launch day. Most of all, just like a happy employee, a happy ARC reader that feels appreciated, will offer free publicity about your book and you as an author. They will share their experience with their friends and family which will lead to future ARC readers and fans.

All Reviews Are Good Reviews

By far the biggest mistake I see the majority of authors, unintentionally make, in regards to getting reviews is to include limiting words in their review 'message'. Saying things like "If you liked this book, please leave a review…" automatically limits your pool of possible reviews. Getting a reader to take the time to write a review for your book is hard enough, so WHY reduce your chances even further by putting stipulations on whether or not they can leave you a review?

This misconception that only 4 and 5 star reviews are valuable to an author is completely outdated. While, yes, 4 and 5 star reviews are what every author hopes for, there are numerous positives to getting lower star reviews as well. To begin with, in the society we live in today, customers are reluctant to trust a product, books included, that only has 5 star ratings. After years of authors having friends and family create reviews for them, the end user has become suspicious of books that look 'too good to be true'. I've known authors who have over 20 reviews, all 5 stars, that complain that although they have a great book, they're getting very little sales. Those same authors have come back to me and told me that after they got a few lower star reviews, their sales picked up.

Don't get me wrong, I'm not saying to go out and ask for low star reviews, but what I am advising is for you to go and ask for HONEST reviews. Asking for honest reviews, but prefacing it with 'If you loved this book..", is not really asking for honest reviews, now is it? Lower rating stars can not only help you, but as in the example above, can actually help restart your books momentum. By changing your wording to simply, "I love to hear from my readers. Let me know what you thought of this book.", can drastically open up your potential for reviews.

Besides opening up your range of people willing to review your book, having lower star ratings can help you grow as an author. It's like when you were in school and took a test. The questions you got right were great, but it was the questions that you missed, that you truly learned from. I suggest reviewing your book reviews, in detail, about once a month, paying close attention to the 3, 2 and 1 star reviews. Often times the reviewer will provide important information as to what they disliked about the book. Perhaps there were a lot of typos that they found throughout the book. In other instances it's possible that they found holes in your plot, under-developed characters or other writing based issues with your story. In any of these cases, you can use this information to improve your writing for future projects. In addition, since we live in such a digital age, in many cases you can use these reviews to fix your current manuscript and just re-publish it as a new edition.

Remember, these people are taking the time to provide real feedback about your book, so don't let that information go to waste. Use it to better yourself and your product. Now, of course, you will still get the occasional negative reviews that you completely disagree with, and that's fine. Whatever you do, do NOT engage in arguments or 'heated discussions' or in any other way respond to these reviews. Just let them be. Positive or negative, these reviews are helping you. Platforms like Amazon use your NUMBER of reviews and not so much your overall rating, in their algorithm to determine where you show up on search results. So by simply tweaking your verbiage when you ask for reviews, can help increase your total number of reviews, help you grow as an author and help you rank better in search results, all of which lead to greater exposure and more potential sales.

How To Follow Up

I touched on this a bit in a previous chapter, but simply asking for reviews is not enough in this busy world we live in. Everyone is running around with a phone attached to them at all times. It's not that people don't care; ok, maybe some people don't care, but in general your readers want to help you, they just need to be reminded. As with most things in life, there is a right and a wrong way to handle this.

Just like the title of this book states, you do not want to come off like you're begging for reviews. There should be a logical and systematic way for you to follow-up with potential reviewers. The most important tool for any organized process is a system of data collection. In the case of reviewers, this system can simply be a spreadsheet. On the spreadsheet you'll want to list the readers name, what format of the book they received from you, the source from which you met them, how you contacted them and the date that they received the book. While this may not sound like a lot of information, these key elements will tell you everything you need to know to help you organize your review reminders. Right after the date field I'd suggest creating three more fields, 'Conf.', 'Rem1' and 'Rem2'. More on these in a moment.

The readers name is obviously information you need. You want this so that you can personalize your review inquiry reminders. You have a much better chance of a positive outcome if the reminders are personal as oppose to just a generic auto-response request. For this same reason, you want to collect the format the reviewer received the book in to further personalize the request. You don't want to just list 'digital copy', instead, list specifics. Was it a pdf, a doc, a mobi or epub file? These specifics will help you especially if you find a commonality. Perhaps everyone who got an .epub file is having problems opening it. This will help you pinpoint issues and possibly explain reasons why they're not reviewing your book. They can't review it if they can't open it.

The source that you met the reader in could be that they were from your email list or perhaps you met them in a social media group or forum. I have found the results from the source field to be extremely helpful information, not only for review reminders, but also if you find that there are certain groups or forums that you're getting a greater response from, you can be sure to stay engaged with that group to broaden your author platform for future books. This field may be the same or slightly differ from the 'contact' column. For example, I may have met someone through a Facebook group and sent them a .pdf copy of my book through messenger while another person I met through that same group, I emailed them a .mobi version of the book. If you sent it via email, you want to make sure you write down that email address. How you sent it to them will be the same way that you will reach out to them later to make your review reminder.

Finally, we come to one of the most important pieces of information in your spreadsheet, the date you sent them the file. Whether you mailed them a physical book or you sent them a digital copy, you want to write down that date. This leads us to those last three fields. 'Conf' will be your confirmation info. This could be a check mark or a date. In either case, after you send out the copy of the book, you want to follow back up and confirm the reader received what you sent. Obviously, if you sent out a physical copy of the book you will most likely want to wait a week or so to ensure it has been delivered and intact. If there are any issues, you want to try and address them as you do not want delays in delivery to cost you, either resulting in a negative review or no review at all.

After you've confirmed that the book has been received, sit back and relax. Give the reader ample time to read your book. Also, remember that people read at different speeds as well as have different distractions in their lives. I have read a 500 page novel in one day while other times it's taken me a week to read a 200 page book. So give people an adequate amount of time to read and digest your book. Depending on the length, I would say wait anywhere between 2-3 weeks after confirmation that they received your book before you follow up and see if they've reviewed it.

If they have not, see if there are any literary issues they're running into and if so, try to address them. If not, thank them and tell them you'll check back in in a few weeks. In the 'Rem1' field put the date that you sent that first reminder. Then wait another 2-3 weeks and follow up again. Put the date of this second follow up in the 'Rem2' field.

Now, how you word your follow up is extremely important. You don't want to email them or message them on social media and say something like, "hey, did you review my book yet." This is a great way to ensure you do NOT get a review from this person. Instead, you want to be sincere and polite. You're not CHECKING UP on them, your CHECKING IN on them. There's a big difference! So, the way you want to address it is, "I wanted to see if you had a chance to read my book. I'm really excited to hear what you thought about..." This will go a long way with readers. If they have started the book but haven't had a chance to finish, ask them what they like and don't like so far. Again, you're making them feel needed and appreciated. This interest will drive them to want to finish the story so that you can get their full opinion of the story.

Perhaps they haven't even started it. Make sure they know that you understand that life is hectic and that you can't wait to hear what they think about your story. Again, showing more interest in them than you do in yourself will drastically help your chances of getting a final review from them. If at any point in your reminder follow ups you find out that they left you a review, make sure you thank them. While you're at it, if they enjoyed your book ask them if they'd be interested in being an ARC reader for your next book.

You may find that even after two rounds of reminders some people still have not reviewed your book. In cases like that, just reiterate that you understand how crazy busy life is. Try to probe and see if there's anything in the story itself that has made finishing it difficult. Let them know that you're really interested in what they thought and that you can't wait for their valued feedback. And then, let it go. After you've done your second reminder, people are either going to review it, or they won't. There's nothing more you can do. You may want to make an asterisk by their name so you know to be a little more reluctant to send them a copy next time. Who knows, sometimes things come up and they can't get around to reading and reviewing it this time, but for your next book, they may do great. Typically, I wait until someone has burnt me twice before I put them on my do not send list. That said, if they've burnt me once before, while I will still send them a copy of the book, it will only be a digital copy. I will not send out another physical copy until they've followed through on multiple books reviews.

How To Give A Good Review

Authors are constantly asking how to get more reviews for their books. While I completely understand the desire to get more reviews since so many platform's algorithms focus on number of reviews when determining the books placement on the page, what I've found is that most people, authors included, don't know how to give a good review.

To be clear, when I say 'how to give a good review' I don't mean 'good' in the sense of a positive review. Instead, I mean how to give a useful review. A review with substance. There can be a negative review that still has substance. While I've seen 5 star reviews that are completely vague and useless. There are a few key parts that make up a 'good' review and once you know how to give a 'good' review, you'll know how to guide others into giving a more useful review of your books.

The most important part of a good review is in its details. Whether you like the book or not you want to give useful, specific details on what you thought of it. If there were a lot of typos, state that. If there were plot holes in the story, make sure you specify what was lacking. Now, this is not to say that you should give away spoilers of the book. Nothing is more annoying to a reader than to read a review and already know the plot and possible ending of the story.

If you liked the book, state what you enjoyed about it. Did you like the fact that it was written in first person point of view? Perhaps the relationship between the main characters brought out some nostalgic feelings. If there were illustrations, you can state how the colorful or whimsical images enhanced the story. Whatever the case, you can provide insightful details without giving away any valuable story information. Remember that a potential customer is reading the review to help them decide on whether that book is something they will enjoy and if it is worth the purchase. If they want to know about the story line, they can read the book description. The job of the reviewer is to simply give their views of the book based on their reading experience.

There are some platforms that add a flag of sorts on reviews from people who purchased the book directly through their platform. Unfortunately, this gives a negative connotation to those books that were acquired other ways. Some may have been purchased on other platforms, at book signings, won in a giveaway or given as a gift. In all of these instances, these would not be flagged as 'purchases' on reviews on some sites. Because the average consumer does not understand this flagging system, it is imperative that when someone acquires a book in one of the other ways, that they denote this in their review. This way the reader of the review knows that it's not just a made up review. The book was acquired elsewhere and then reviewed on that platform. For example, if someone bought one of your books at a book signing, you'd want them to state, "I got this book when the author was signing books in [city]..." this adds a great deal of authenticity to that review. Even if you gave the book out to an ARC reader, they can say, "I was lucky enough to get an advanced copy of this book..." Both of these examples, while not labeled as a 'purchase' by some platforms, give enough information to reassure the potential customer that this is an authentic review.

10 Out-Of-The-Box Ideas
For Getting Reviews

Ok, so you've survived through the other chapters, been inundated with information and hopefully learned a few things along the way. As a reward for your patience and your desire to work smarter to get book reviews, I have listed 10 not-so-normal ways to find book reviews.

1. **Ask for video reviews** – People see written book reviews on platforms everywhere, but how often have you seen a video review. While not super common, yet, these reviews can be extremely helpful as they relay to a potential customer the actual emotion behind a review. Seeing the smile on someone's face as they talk about the book or the tear in their eye as they remember a specific scene, these are elements that are lost in a written review.

2. **Take offline reviews and put them online** – I touched on this a bit in an earlier chapter, but you should reach out to local newspapers, book clubs, etc and ask them to review your book. Then take a picture of that written review and share it on your website and all of your social media. Also post them on your Amazon Central and Goodreads author pages.

3. **<u>Reach out to librarians</u>** – Both public and school librarians are a great resource. You can give them a free copy of your book and then tell them that if they like it, you can give them another copy that they can give out to one of their patrons.

4. **<u>Go review hunting</u>** – Find books that are similar to yours and check out their reviews. If you find a good 4 or 5 star review, try to reach out to the reviewer and tell them, "I saw your great review of [competitor's book]. Since you liked that book, I thought you'd might like to check out a copy of my book…"

5. **<u>Bring your book to life</u>** – Put your book up on audio. Depending on where you publish it through, I know there are some platforms that offer you FREE promo codes to the audio version that you can send out for promotional purposes. When you send out these free codes be sure to mention how you'd love their feedback.

6. **<u>Be professional</u>** – Just like with any business, have business cards or better yet, bookmarks, made up that includes your importance of reviews 'message' and include them in all of your business dealings. The bookmarks are extremely useful at book signings or when you mail out copies of your book.

7. **<u>Get in the giving mood</u>** – Find a local organization that is having a banquet or auction and offer up some copies of your books to be included in one of the baskets. If there's no basket that it fits in with, make one. A coffee mug, some tea bags, fragrance candles, bubble bath and a copy of your book would make a great 'escape' basket. Don't forget to include your specially made bookmark to the basket.

8. **<u>No more wasted space</u>** – As stated earlier in the book, use the blank space on your copyright page to place a review reminder. This way even if they don't finish your book, they've already been introduced to the idea of giving a review.

9. **<u>Stick together</u>** – Try to get another author to review your book, you can then take that review and place it as an editorial review on your books description page. It doesn't matter if that author is from the same genre or not. In addition to making your book stand out more, this also introduces you to the fans of the other author.

10. **<u>Reinvent the wheel</u>** – Create a 'Review Wheel'. A review wheel is different than an author review swap in that the author of the book you're reviewing will NOT be the author reviewing your book. In the simplest of terms, Author A reviews the book of Author B. Author B reviews the book of Author C and, you guessed it, Author C reviews the book of Author A. This way there are no feelings of reciprocity and honest reviews are more natural.

My goal with this list is to help ignite a spark within you to think outside of the box in regards to drumming up some real, organic reviews.

Conclusion

I spent this entire book providing you with insights as to the who, when, where and why's when it comes to getting organic book reviews. With all of that being said, if there is nothing else that you take away from this book, I hope you remember this; reviews are not the magic bullet to success. The best way to increase your book sales and your popularity is to write more books. As I've said numerous times throughout this book, it's a numbers game. The more books you write, the better your chances of being discovered by readers. Now, the quality of those books will determine if those readers turn into fans.

Let's be honest, you most likely did not get into the book writing and publishing business to get rich, quick. With that in mind, just remember why you started writing in the first place and focus on your craft. Utilize the tools I've given you to get more organic, useful reviews. Then take the feedback you get from those reviews and use them to perfect your craft!

<u>The best of luck to you and your books!</u>

About The Author

International #1 bestselling author, Keith Wheeler, was born in Danbury, CT. His maternal grandmother was a published poet, so Keith was surrounded by writing and the love of reading from an early age. At the age of 9, Keith and his family moved from Connecticut to a small town just outside of Daytona Beach, FL. While still a freshman in high school, he had his first piece of work published. It was a poem that he'd written for his 9th grade English class. As a huge coincidence, Keith's grandmother was published in that exact same book. From that point on, he knew it was a sign that he was meant to write. After graduation he would marry his high school sweetheart, Suzette. They currently reside in southwest Missouri where they raise their four children. Keith continues to write, with projects ranging from children's picture books to softball-themed journals. In addition to publishing over a dozen of his own books, Keith has also helped other writers accomplish their dreams of being published authors. To date, Keith has helped published over 30 books, with no plans to stop anytime soon.

I'd love your HONEST feedback!

Let me know what you thought

of this book!

https://www.amazon.com/dp/B0795FHPV8